# ALPHA BOOKS

# RIVERS, PONDS AND LAKES

## NICOLA BARBER

Evans

## EVANS BROTHERS LIMITED

First published 1993
Reprinted 1995

Typeset by Fleetlines Typesetters, Southend-on-Sea
Printed in Spain by GRAFO, S.A. – Bilbao

ISBN 0 237 51323 4

# Acknowledgements

Editor: Su Swallow
Language advisor: Suzanne Tiburtius (East Kent Integrated Support Service)
Design: Neil Sayer
Production: Jenny Mulvanny

Illustrations: David Gardner, Graeme Chambers
Maps: Hardlines, Charlbury

For permission to reproduce copyright material the author and publishers gratefully acknowledge the following:

**Cover** (Okavango Delta) Gerald Cubitt, Bruce Coleman Limited
**Title page** (Bangladesh) Mark Edwards, Still Pictures

**p5** (top) Ron Cartmell, Bruce Coleman Limited, (bottom) Phillippe Henry, Oxford Scientific Films **p6** (main) Ake Lindau/Okapia, Oxford Scientific Films, (inset) Ronald Toms, Oxford Scientific Films **p7** (left) G. Ziesler, Bruce Coleman Limited, (right) Konrad Wothe, Bruce Coleman Limited **p8** NASA/Science Photo Library **p9** John Shaw, NHPA **p10** N. A. Callow, NHPA **p11** Martin Wendler, NHPA **p13** George McCarthy, Bruce Coleman Limited, (inset) Dr Eckart Pott, Bruce Coleman Limited **p14** (top) Martin Wendler, NHPA, (bottom left) David Woodfall, NHPA, (right) Michael Freeman, Bruce Coleman Limited **p15** Mark Edwards, Still Pictures **p16** Haroldo Palo, NHPA **p17** (top) Mark Edwards, Still Pictures, (bottom) Mark Carwardine, Biotica **p18**

Hans Reinhard, Bruce Coleman Limited **p19** Gerald Cubitt, Bruce Coleman Limited **p20** (left) Gerald Cubitt, Bruce Coleman Limited, (right) Dieter and Mary Plage, Bruce Coleman Limited **p21** Sally Morgan/ECOSCENE **p22** Harold Taylor ABIPP, Oxford Scientific Films **p23** (top) Jane Burton, Bruce Coleman Limited, (bottom) Kim Taylor, Bruce Coleman Limited **p24** Jane Burton, Bruce Coleman Limited **p25** (top) M. P. L. Fogden, Bruce Coleman Limited, (bottom) Jane Burton, Bruce Coleman Limited **p27** Peter Hulme/ECOSCENE, (inset) Sally Morgan/ECOSCENE **p28** Jeff Foott, Bruce Coleman Limited **p29** Gordon Langsbury, Bruce Coleman Limited **p30** (top) Richard Kirby, Oxford Scientific Films, (bottom) Doug Allan, Oxford Scientific Films **p31** Peter Davey ARPS, Bruce Coleman Limited **p32** Peter Davey ARPS, Bruce Coleman Limited **p33** Jane Burton, Bruce Coleman Limited **p34** Gerald Cubitt, Bruce Coleman Limited **p35** (left) Bruce Coleman Limited, (right) Nigel Dennis NHPA **p36** (top) Jack Dermid, Oxford Scientific Films, (bottom) B. Kloske/ECOSCENE **p37** Winkley/ECOSCENE **p38** Sorensen and Olsen, NHPA **p39** (top) Mark N. Boulton, Bruce Coleman Limited, (bottom) Mark Edwards, Still Pictures **p41** Gerald Cubitt, Bruce Coleman Limited **p42** Michael Freeman, Bruce Coleman Limited **p43** D. and R. Sullivan, Bruce Coleman Limited, (inset) Sullivan and Rogers, Bruce Coleman Limited **p44** Mark Edwards, Still Pictures

# Contents

# Introduction

Water covers about two thirds of the surface of the earth. Most of this water is salty. This salty water makes up the seas and oceans. Some of the water covering the earth is not salty. This is called freshwater. Over three quarters of all the freshwater on earth is frozen into ice caps. These huge ice caps cover the Arctic and Antarctic. The rest of the freshwater lies in rivers, lakes, ponds and swamps. There is also freshwater under the ground.

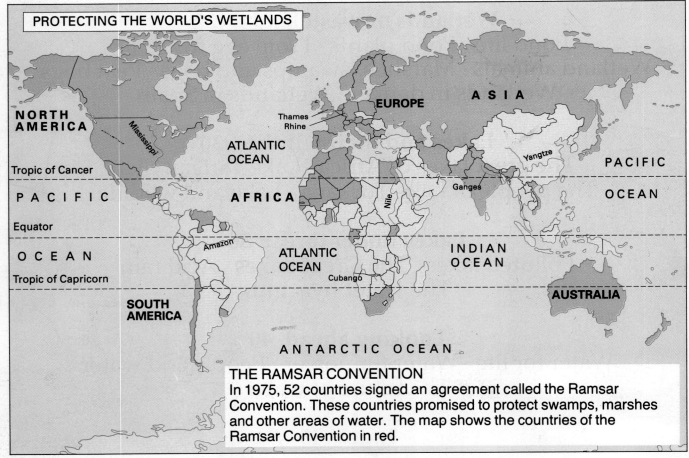

PROTECTING THE WORLD'S WETLANDS

NORTH AMERICA
Mississippi
ATLANTIC OCEAN
Tropic of Cancer
PACIFIC
Equator
OCEAN
Tropic of Capricorn
Amazon
SOUTH AMERICA
AFRICA
Nile
ATLANTIC OCEAN
Cubangó
EUROPE
Thames
Rhine
ASIA
Yangtze
Ganges
PACIFIC
OCEAN
INDIAN OCEAN
AUSTRALIA
ANTARCTIC OCEAN

THE RAMSAR CONVENTION
In 1975, 52 countries signed an agreement called the Ramsar Convention. These countries promised to protect swamps, marshes and other areas of water. The map shows the countries of the Ramsar Convention in red.

△ The River Nile at Cairo, in Egypt

People get their drinking water from rivers, ponds and lakes. Farmers water their fields to make their crops grow. Factories are built on river banks so that they can use the river water. But water is often polluted (made dirty) by waste and chemicals. Pollution affects the animals and plants that live in or near water. Many animals and plants die every year because of polluted water. All over the world, people are working to clean up dirty rivers, ponds and lakes.

◁ The grey heron lives near rivers and lakes.

# Flowing freshwater

## From mountain to sea

Most rivers start as little streams, high up in the mountains. As a stream flows downhill it is joined by many other small streams. By now, the water in the stream is flowing so fast that it can carry rocks with it.

▽ A fast-flowing stream, and (inset) a slow-moving river.

▽ A dipper dives under water to find food.

△ A torrent duck clings tightly on to a rock.

Most animals find it difficult to live in mountain streams because the water flows so quickly. But the torrent duck lives in streams high in the Andes Mountains of South America. It has claws on its feet so that it can grip tightly on slippery rocks. Another bird that lives in mountain streams is the dipper. It is a skilful swimmer under water.

As the river leaves the hills behind, it starts to slow down. The water now carries mud and sand along with it. Animals such as otters and water voles live in holes along the banks of the river.

7

△ This picture shows what the delta of the River Nile in Egypt looks like from the air.

**The journey's end**
At the end of its long journey, the river comes to the sea. The fresh water in the river meets the salt water of the sea. The place where this happens is called an estuary. In an estuary there are often large flocks of birds, especially wading birds and gulls.

As the river flows into its estuary it drops its load of mud and sand. The piles of mud and sand build up to make new land. This new land is called a delta. The delta grows bigger, pushing the coastline further out to sea. The delta of the River Nile in Egypt is shaped like a fan.

The delta of the River Nile is very **fertile**. Many crops and plants grow there. Papyrus plants grow there. The papyrus plant grows very quickly. A huge number of plants can grow in a small space. Thousands of years ago, the Ancient Egyptians used the papyrus plant to make mats, sails and paper. Today, people make the plants into logs to burn for heating and cooking.

**River homes**

Rivers provide homes for many creatures. Some fish do not live in one part of a river all the time. They travel long distances along the river. These long journeys are called migrations. Fish such as salmon make long migrations. They spend part of their lives in a river, and part in the sea.

▽ Salmon sometimes have to leap up waterfalls on their long migrations.

△ A papyrus plant

## Leaping salmon

Salmon lay their eggs at the bottom of a fast-flowing stream. After the young salmon have hatched from their eggs, they live in the stream for two or three years. They then migrate to the sea. They stay in the sea for about four years. The salmon then go back to the stream where they were born to lay their eggs. As they swim from the sea up the river, they sometimes have to leap over waterfalls. Some salmon can swim as far as 115 kilometres every day.

△ Pollution in a river in Austria

## River pollution

Many salmon are killed by **pollution** in the river water. Some rivers in Norway, Wales and Scotland no longer have salmon because they are too dirty. In Poland, the River Vistula is so polluted that no animals or plants can live in its waters. The River Vistula flows into the Baltic Sea. The pollution in the river has spread across the sea. Many grey seals have died because the sea water is also polluted. Around the world, there are many other rivers like the River Vistula.

Much of the pollution in river water comes from farmland.

△ Otters die when they eat poisoned fish.

Many farmers use fertilizers to help their crops to grow. They spread the fertilizers on the soil. Farmers also use pesticides to stop insects and animals damaging their crops. When rain falls on to the fields, it washes the chemicals from the fertilizers and pesticides off the land. The chemicals run into the rivers and poison the fish. Animals such as otters will also die if they eat the poisoned fish.

River pollution does not only come from farmland. Many factories put poisonous waste into rivers. Even fishing by a river can cause pollution. Some fishermen use weights made of lead at the end of their fishing lines. Sometimes a weight falls off. If a swan swallows the weight, the swan will die.

We must begin to take more care of our rivers. If we do not keep them clean, animals and plants will die. Rivers will turn into dirty stretches of water without the wildlife that makes them so special.

△ Beavers build a dam with logs across the shallow part of a river. The dam holds water in a small pool. The beaver builds a shelter, called a lodge, in the pool.

▷ Many swans are killed by lead fishing weights.

**pollution** anything that makes air or water dirty and dangerous to live in. **fertile** describes land that can produce strong, healthy plants.

# Rivers around the world

There are rivers all over the world. There are rivers high up in the mountains, in hot regions, and even in deserts. Rivers provide homes for many plants and animals. Rivers also provide water and food for people. Sadly, people are spoiling rivers in many parts of the world.

## The mighty Amazon

The River Amazon in South America is the world's second longest river, after the River Nile. It is 6437

△ An anaconda squeezes a cayman to death. A cayman is a kind of alligator.

▽ Tropical rainforest grows along the banks of the River Amazon.

△ The piranha fish has teeth as sharp as a razor.

△ The Amazonian water lily has giant leaves.

kilometres long. It flows from the Andes Mountains in Peru, through the Amazon rainforest, to the Atlantic Ocean in northern Brazil.

Over 2000 different types of fish live in the River Amazon. The fiercest fish is the piranha. The piranha is not very big – it only grows up to 60 centimetres long. But it has a mouth full of razor-sharp teeth. The piranha uses its teeth to attack and eat other animals and fish.

Many animals come to the river to drink. They must watch out for anacondas. The anaconda is the largest snake in the world. It kills other animals by squeezing them. It then swallows them whole.

One of the biggest plants in the world lives in the River Amazon. The Amazonian water lily has giant leaves. They can measure up to 1.5 metres across. They float on the surface of the water.

△ An Amazonian manatee

## The Amazon in danger

Many rare animals live in or near the River Amazon.

The Amazonian manatee is found only in the River Amazon. It does not live anywhere else in the world. In the past, people killed many thousands of manatees for their meat. Manatees are now protected. This means that no one is allowed to kill manatees.

The biggest threat to the River Amazon is the destruction of the Amazon rainforest. Each year, people cut down a huge area of this rainforest. Some of the land is used for mining. Waste from the mines pollutes the river. We must try to stop the destruction of the rainforest in order to protect the River Amazon and its wildlife.

## The River Ganges

The River Ganges is India's main river. It flows down from the Himalayan Mountains. After about 2500 kilometres, it joins the Brahmaputra River in Bangladesh. The two rivers flow through the Bay of Bengal and come out into the Indian Ocean.

The Ganges is a holy river for many Indian people. They visit the river to bathe and pray. The Ganges is also a dirty river. It is polluted by waste from factories and by chemicals from farmland.

The pollution in the Ganges is dangerous for the dolphins that live in the river. There are five different types of river dolphin in the world. They are all threatened by pollution. The Baiji river dolphin lives in the Yangtze River in China. Many Baiji river dolphins are killed when they are hit by boats on the river.

△ People visit the Ganges River to bathe and pray.

▽ The Baiji river dolphin lives in the Yangtze River in China.

## Mangrove forest

The mangrove is a type of tree that can grow in wet, swampy areas. The biggest mangrove forest in the world is called the Sundarbans. It lies in the delta of the Ganges and Brahmaputra rivers. The Sundarbans mangrove forest stretches for almost 6000 kilometres. It is home to many different types of fish and shellfish. The Royal Bengal tiger also lives there. The tiger is a protected animal in the Sundarbans.

△ Tigers are protected animals in the Sundarbans.

## Dangerous floods

The delta of the Ganges and Brahmaputra rivers in Bangladesh is very fertile. Many people live in the delta and grow crops in the fertile soil. But the delta is often flooded by the sea during bad storms. In 1990, at least 200,000 people drowned in floodwaters in Bangladesh. The mangrove forests help to protect the coast during storms.

△ The delta of the
Okavango River

## The Okavango Delta

The River Okavango in Africa flows
from mountains in Angola into
northern Botswana. The River
Okavango does not flow out into the
sea. Instead, it sinks into the sands of
the Kalahari Desert. The river forms
a huge inland delta. In the delta, the
river divides up into thousands of
streams, with islands in-between.

## Animals of the Okavango

A large variety of animals lives in the Okavango Delta. Many birds live there. The malachite kingfisher is a tiny bird. When the male malachite kingfisher looks for a mate he offers her bits of fish. Both the male and female help to make the nest. When the eggs hatch, both parents look after the new chicks.

The Pel's fishing owl hunts at night and rests during the day. The owl has large eyes for seeing in the dark. At night, it perches in a low branch over the river. The owl drops into the water when it sees a fish. It picks up the fish with its feet.

▽ The Pel's fishing owl hunts at night.

▷ A malachite kingfisher

20

## Okavango under threat

In December 1990, part of the Okavango Delta came under threat. The owners of the world's largest diamond mine wanted to drain the water away from part of the delta. They wanted to use the water in the mine. But this plan would have killed many of the animals living in the delta. Many people protested about the plan. They wanted to stop the mine owners draining the delta. Work did stop in March 1991. Now people hope that the Okavango Delta is safe for the future.

## A worldwide problem

Rivers in different countries have different problems. But they are all in danger from pollution. Many people are now working to clean up the world's rivers. People are also helping to protect areas like the Amazon rainforest and the Okavango Delta.

▽ The River Rhine is badly polluted, but people are trying to clean it up.

# Wetlands or wastelands?

△ Mallard ducks often nest beside ponds.

Ponds, swamps, bogs and marshes are often known as wetlands. Many thousands of different animals and plants live in the world's wetlands. Sadly, pollution often affects wetlands. People dump rubbish in them. Sometimes people drain wetlands to make more dry land.

## Pond life

A huge number of tiny animals live in a pond. Many of these animals are too small for humans to see. Insects such as water fleas live on plant leaves, in the spaces between grains of sand, and underneath stones. Shellfish and worms live in the mud at the bottom of the pond.

## Pond plants

Many plants grow around the edge of a pond. They are called marginal plants. They include irises, marsh marigolds and rushes. Marginal plants provide food and shelter for many animals.

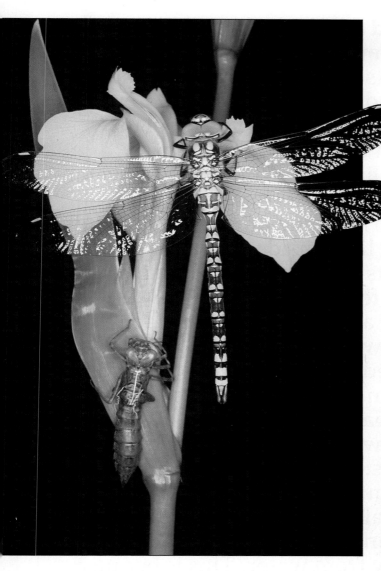

△ This dragonfly has just come out of its nymph skin.

Other plants grow in the water of the pond. The leaves of a water lily float on the surface of the water. The lily's roots grow into the mud at the bottom of the pond. Some floating water plants do not have any roots. Duckweeds and bladderworts do not have roots. They grow across the surface of the pond. They look like a thick green blanket lying on top of the pond.

**From egg to adult**
Some animals start life in the pond, but when they grow up they leave the water. A dragonfly begins as an egg laid in the water. The egg hatches into an insect called a nymph. The nymph spends two years in the water while it grows bigger. Then it crawls up a plant stem to the surface of the pond. It pushes off its skin and turns into a dragonfly.

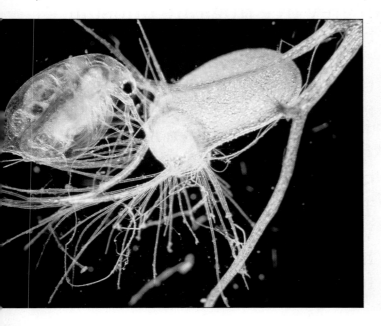

◁ Bladderworts eat tiny water animals.

23

## Wetland animals

Many unusual animals live in wetlands. The water spider is the only spider that can live in water. It spins a web of silk between plant stems in the water. The web is shaped like a large bubble. The water spider carries air from the surface down to its home until the web is full of air. It lives inside its web. It only leaves its web to collect more air, and to hunt for insects and fish.

Some animals spend half their lives in water, and half on land. They are called amphibians. Frogs, toads, newts and salamanders are all amphibians. Female frogs lay their eggs in water. The eggs hatch into tadpoles. The tadpoles live in the water until they grow legs and turn into small frogs. Then they move on to the land. But frogs never go very far away from water. This is because they must keep their skins damp in order to breathe.

▽ The water spider lives in a bubble of air inside a web.

African grey tree frogs are unusual because they do not lay their eggs in water. Instead, they find a tree branch that is growing over some water. The female makes a special foam nest on the branch. She lays the eggs in the foam. The foam keeps the eggs wet. When the eggs hatch, the tadpoles drop out of the foam into the water below.

△ African grey tree frogs make a foam nest.

The axolotl is another unusual amphibian. It is unusual because it spends its whole life in the water. It grows up to 25 centimetres long, but it never changes from being a tadpole. The axolotl is a kind of salamander.

◁ The axolotl is a kind of salamander.

## Marshes, swamps and bogs

If a pond begins to dry up, it becomes marsh or swamp. This often happens when the plants around the edge of a pond start to grow into the middle. The thick roots of the plants grow through the muddy ground and up into the water. They send up new shoots in the water. Bit by bit the flow of the water slows down, and the pond turns into a marsh or a swamp.

Marshes and swamps provide homes for many different kinds of birds. Bitterns and reed warblers live among the reed stems. They feed on insects and build nests out of reeds.

## Peat bogs

**Peat** bogs are like marshes and swamps in the way they form. Peat bogs are made out of a type of moss, called sphagnum moss. The sphagnum moss gradually grows across the water. This moss can soak up huge amounts of water. When the moss dies it does not rot away completely because it contains so much water. Instead, it builds up in layers. In the end, these layers turn into peat. It can take over 5000 years for a peat bog to form. Plants such as pennyworts, bog pimpernels and bog asphodel all grow in peat bogs.

▷ Bog asphodel (inset) grows in peat bogs. This peat bog is in Scotland.

## Wetlands in danger

People have probably destroyed about half the wetlands of the world. Rubbish is thrown into ponds. Marshes and swamps are drained to make new land for building or farming. Almost half the wetlands in the USA have been turned into farmland.

The most famous area of wetlands in the USA is the Everglades in Florida. The Everglades is a huge area of swamps. It includes the Kissimmee River and Lake Okeechobee. Since the 1900s, people have drained many of the swamps in the Everglades for farmland. Chemicals from the fields have polluted the lake. These changes put the wildlife in the Everglades in danger.

Farmers also take water from the Everglades to put on their crops. But in 1988 there was a bad **drought** in the USA. People began to realise that they must protect the Everglades, not only for the wildlife, but also for their own water supply. Now there are new rules that stop people taking too much water out of the swamps.

△ Alligators in the Everglades, Florida, USA

## Wetlands in Spain

The Coto Doñana National Park in Spain is an area of wetland. About 10,000 flamingoes live there, as well as otters, lynx and eagles. Many other birds stop in the Coto Doñana wetlands as they migrate between Europe and Africa.

Farmers use water from the Coto Doñana wetlands to put on their farmland. Many tourists also visit the area. There are plans to build more hotels and golf courses near the wetlands. If these plans go ahead, much of the wildlife in the wetlands will probably die out.

△ Flamingoes live in the Coto Doñana National Park.

△ The wood stork lives in the Everglades.

**peat** dark brown, rotting plant material, found in cool, wet places.
**drought** a long period of little or no rainfall.

29

# Lakes and their wildlife

Lakes can change shape and get smaller, just like ponds. The water in a lake comes from streams, rivers and rainfall. The mud and sand carried by rivers can fill up a shallow lake. But some lakes are so deep that this is not a problem. Lake Baikal in Russia, and Lake Victoria in Africa are both very deep lakes. Lake Baikal is the deepest lake in the world. It measures 1742 metres at its deepest point. Lake Baikal is home to the only freshwater seal in the world. It is called the Baikal seal. There are about 70,000 seals living in Lake Baikal.

△ Lake Baikal, Russia

▽ A Baikal seal

△ Lake Magadi is one of the soda lakes in the Great Rift Valley in Africa.

## The great lakes of Africa

Lake Victoria is one of the many lakes in the Great Rift Valley in Africa. The valley is a huge crack in the earth. It was formed millions of years ago by movements of the ground. The Great Rift Valley runs from Lebanon in the Middle East to Mozambique in the south. The valley is about 6500 kilometres long.

Many of the lakes in the Great Rift Valley are full of a mineral called soda. Soda is used to make glass and soap. Every year, about half a million tonnes of soda are taken from Lake Magadi in Kenya. The soda is then sold abroad.

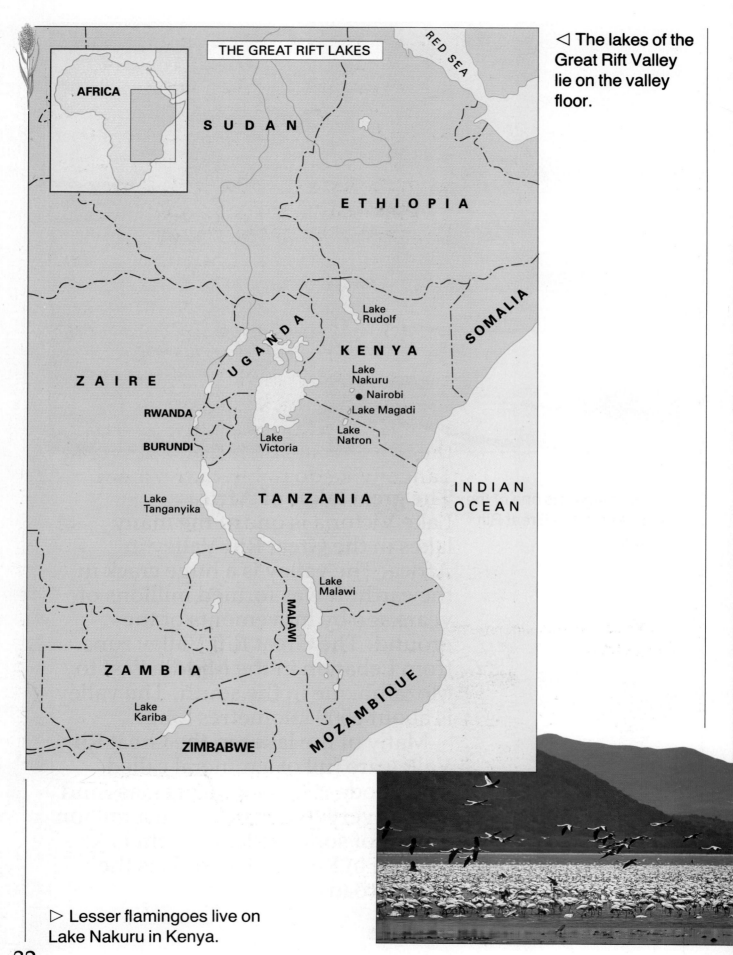

THE GREAT RIFT LAKES

AFRICA

RED SEA

S U D A N

E T H I O P I A

Lake
Rudolf

U G A N D A

K E N Y A

S O M A L I A

Z A I R E

Lake
Nakuru

● Nairobi

Lake Magadi

RWANDA

BURUNDI

Lake
Victoria

Lake
Natron

Lake
Tanganyika

T A N Z A N I A

INDIAN
OCEAN

Lake
Malawi

MALAWI

Z A M B I A

Lake
Kariba

M O Z A M B I Q U E

ZIMBABWE

◁ The lakes of the
Great Rift Valley
lie on the valley
floor.

▷ Lesser flamingoes live on
Lake Nakuru in Kenya.

Lake Nakuru is in Kenya in Africa. It is a soda lake. The lake is full of tiny shrimps and other water animals. These animals provide food for huge flocks of lesser flamingoes. The flamingoes get their pink colour from the food that they eat. If they stopped eating shrimps, the flamingoes would turn grey.

## Lake Tanganyika

Lake Tanganyika is the deepest lake in Africa. Its deepest point measures about 1400 metres. The lake is many millions of years old.

Lake Tanganyika has its own special collection of animals. Many of the fish and shellfish that live in Lake Tanganyika do not live anywhere else in the world. Two thirds of all the fish that live in the lake are called cichlids. Cichlids take great care of their babies. Most fish lay their eggs and then leave them. But cichlids guard their eggs until they have hatched. Then they look after the young fish. One type of cichlid fish is called the mouthbrooder. The female mouthbrooder guards her young fish in her mouth until they can look after themselves.

▽ Cichlids take great care of their young.

△ The Turkana hang up fish to dry.

## The people of Lake Turkana
The people that live along the shores of Lake Turkana are called the Turkana. They catch fish from the lake to eat, and to sell. Much of the water in Lake Turkana comes from the River Omo. The River Omo flows from Ethiopia. But the River Omo is drying up because of a long drought in Ethiopia. So the lake is getting smaller. The Turkana can no longer catch as many fish. They have to find other ways of making a living.

## Lakeland wildlife

Many animals live in lakes and around the edges of lakes. They are often specially adapted to help them live in or on the water. For example, the African jacana has big feet. Its toes are up to eight centimetres long. The jacana uses its big feet to walk across the water lily leaves and other plants that float on the surface of a lake. As it walks, it catches insects and small fish for food.

The duck-billed platypus lives in streams, rivers and lakes in Australia. It eats insects, worms and shellfish. When it is under water, the platypus closes its eyes and ears to stop the water getting in. The platypus finds its way around by its sense of touch.

▽ The African jacana walks across water lily leaves.

▽ A duck-billed platypus

# Lakes under threat

Many lakes are threatened by pollution. Like rivers and wetlands, lakes are polluted by waste from factories, and by chemicals in pesticides and fertilizers. People also use lakes for boating and other pastimes. Some people who use the lakes throw rubbish into the water.

## Polluted lakes

Pollution from fertilizers is a big problem in lakes. The chemicals in the fertilizers provide food for tiny plants called **algae**. The fertilizers make the algae grow more quickly than normal. The algae spread across the surface of the water. The thick layer of algae stops sunlight reaching the plants below the surface. In the end, the plants and animals in the lake begin to die.

△ Green algae covers the surface of a pond.

△ Fish often die in polluted lakes and rivers.

△ The city of Toronto lies on the shore of Lake Ontario, one of the five Great Lakes.

## The Great Lakes

The Great Lakes are on the border of Canada and the USA. The five lakes are called Superior, Michigan, Erie, Huron and Ontario. Some of the world's main industrial cities lie on the shores of the lakes.

The St Lawrence River connects the Great Lakes to the Atlantic Ocean. There are many factories on the banks of the river. Waste from these factories has polluted the river. The water is so dirty that it is unsafe for fish, animals and people. The beluga whale lives in the polluted water of the St Lawrence estuary. Every month, the pollution kills one beluga whale. There is a danger that the beluga whale could soon die out.

### Acid rain

Acid rain is caused by smoke and fumes from factory chimneys and car exhausts. Gases in the smoke and fumes rise into the air. The gases mix with water in the clouds to form acid rain. The acid rain falls back to earth. It poisons lakes and rivers, and kills plants such as trees.

The wind can blow the gases from smoke and fumes a very long way. Acid rain often falls far away from the place where the smoke and fumes are. This means that pollution in the USA can cause acid rain in Canada. Smoke and fumes from Great Britain can cause acid rain in Scandinavia. The acid rain poisons the lakes. Many lakes in Norway are so acid that all their fish have died.

△ Thousands of lakes in Norway and Sweden are affected by acid rain.

## The water hyacinth
The water hyacinth grows quickly. It often blocks up rivers and lakes. But it can also be a useful plant. Water hyacinths absorb the harmful chemicals from fertilizers. This leaves the water around the plants pure. Water hyacinths could be used to clean up polluted lakes.

◁ A helicopter sprays lime powder over a polluted lake in Sweden.

Many countries are now trying to clean up their polluted lakes. In Sweden, helicopters spread lime powder on polluted lakes. The lime powder helps to get rid of the acid in the water. But the lime can also damage plants and animals. And the lakes must be sprayed often for the powder to work.

**algae** plants that grow in water. They have no roots, stems or leaves.

# Looking ahead

People need freshwater to live. People drink water, wash in water, and cook with water. Farmers put water on their crops to make them grow. Industry uses a lot of water. Running water can be used to make electricity. People swim, sail and fish in lakes and rivers. For all these reasons, we must look after our freshwater supply.

**Water for life**
In some countries there is plenty of water. People in these countries can turn on the tap and water comes out. One person can use over 500 litres of water every day. In these countries, about half of the freshwater supply is used by industry.

In many of the poorer parts of the world, it is not so easy to get water. People often have to walk a long way to find water. In India, women fetch water from wells. They carry it back to their villages in pots. In India nearly all of the freshwater supply is used for growing food. In these poorer countries, one person uses only two and a half litres of water every day.

In many African and Asian countries, people often have to drink dirty water. Dirty drinking water kills about 25,000 people every day. People die because of germs which are in the water.

Dirty water is also a threat to people in richer countries. In Sweden and Norway, drinking water is affected by acid rain.

▽ Women in India carry water to their village.

## Water for power

Moving water has been used to drive machinery for thousands of years. In the past, people built flour mills next to streams. The streams pushed waterwheels round. The wheels turned the machinery that ground the grain into flour. Today, moving water can be used to make electricity. A dam is built across a river. The dam stops the flow of the river. It holds the water back in a lake, called a reservoir. When pipes in the dam are opened, the water rushes through. The water turns wheels called turbines. The turbines make electricity which is used in our homes, offices and by industry. There are dams all over the world.

▽ The Hoover Dam in Nevada, USA

△ This village sits on an island of reeds on Lake Titicaca.

**People and water**

Water is not only important for drinking and power. For some people, water is part of a way of life. The Indian people of Lake Titicaca live on water. Lake Titicaca is the highest lake in the world. It sits on the border between Bolivia and Peru, high in the Andes Mountains in South America. The Indians build their villages on thick mats made of reeds. The reed mats float on the surface of the lake. The Indians also use reeds for building huts and boats, and for making baskets.

## The future of water

Water is essential for people, animals and plants. In some places there is plenty of clean water. Bhutan is a small country in Asia. There is little industry in Bhutan and the rivers are clean. But in many places, people are polluting rivers, ponds, lakes and wetlands. Luckily, people are trying to clean up the water supplies of the world. It is up to everyone to help to look after the earth's water.

▽ The rivers are clean in Bhutan.

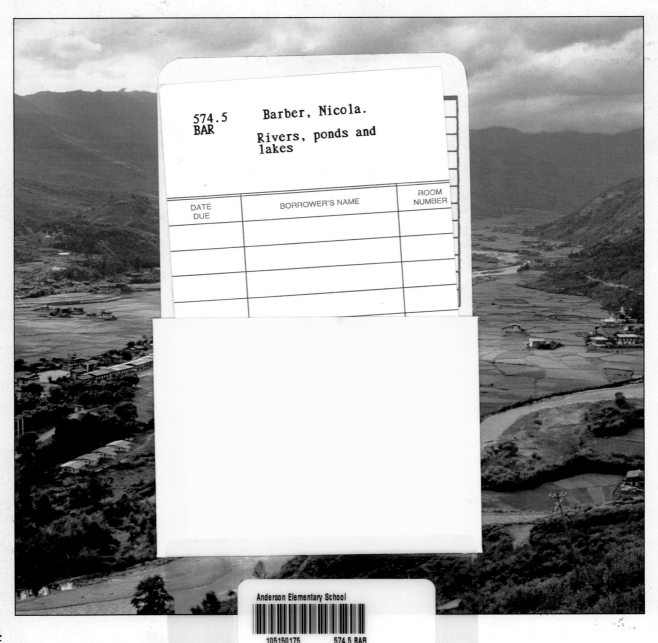